How to Lead Group Bible Study so that People Meet God

Andrew Page

ISBN 978-3-95776-130-9

Cover design: Chris Allcock / VTR Publications

Contents

For all those in the small group
I am part of, including

Becky, Biddy, Jean, Kevin,
Kieran, Lavinia, Mark, Monique
Peter, Richard and Robert

Acknowledgements

I thank God for all those in Austria and the UK to whom I have taught this material in workshops.

I am grateful to Chris Allcock for the cover design and especially to Thomas Mayer for his vision in publishing the book.

A number of people read the manuscript and gave me their comments and suggestions, so I am glad to thank them here: Paul Allcock, David Bacon, Jenny Goon, Gerhild Haitchi, Jo Harkrader, Jack Sivyer, Biddy Taylor and Charlie Watkins.

I wrote *How to Lead Group Bible Study so that People Meet God* during the Covid-19 pandemic of 2020. If the small group you are part of is still meeting online, the book is still relevant (and see the Appendix for a little more help).

I have many friends who have prayed for me in the writing of this book: I owe them a huge debt. Many of them are part of Above Bar Church, Southampton: I would be a lesser person without my church family.

I pray that God will use this material to equip many to lead group Bible study. To him be the glory!

Andrew Page
www.howtoleadgroupbiblestudy.org

Introduction

How to Lead Group Bible Study

The Bible is the word of God. If churches and Christian Unions neglect the word of God, they will not grow and they will not enjoy the relationship they have come into with Jesus.

Here are some basic questions which are designed to get us thinking about the importance of group Bible study as part of a Christian small group. My answers are intended to convince you that this book is worth reading.

And working through.

1. Why do churches and CUs have small groups?

I can think of a number of reasons. They are...

a. A part of the church or CU

If you read the Gospels you will see how Jesus, while teaching and calling the crowds, also had a *small group* consisting of twelve apostles (see Mark 3:13-19). And even within that he had another small group of Peter, James and John (see, for example, Mark 5:37).

Unless your church or Christian Union consists of less than ten people, it makes sense to have small groups. So this is not small group as a *replacement* for church or CU, but small group as *part* of church or CU.

b. A bridge into the church or CU

Sometimes someone's first contact with church or the CU is through a small group: they are a friend of someone in the group. If this proves to be a positive experience, this can make it easier for them to get involved in the larger community.

With others, it's the other way around. Maybe they start with the main meeting and then get invited to join a small group. And that, in turn, helps them to start feeling at home in the wider community.

Whatever the direction, small group can be a bridge between contact with a few people and whole church or CU life.

c. A home in the church or CU

In the main meeting most people don't get the opportunity to be actively engaged. Of course there's sung worship, and conversation beforehand and afterwards, but you can easily feel lost in the crowd.

Potentially the small group solves that problem: here is a meeting designed to enable everyone to contribute in whatever way they feel comfortable.

The small group can be a spiritual home.

2. Why do some people avoid small groups?

Here are some of the reasons.

a. They are too busy

Some parents with young children will struggle to find the time to be part of a small group if it meets in the evening. But having some groups meet during the day may go some way to solving that problem.

b. They are too shy

Some people don't want to speak in a group context. If they think they are going to be forced to do things they don't want to do, they may be very wary of trying a small group.

c. They have had bad small group experiences

Maybe they have been to a small group and the meeting was boring. Or too long. Or unfriendly. Or perhaps the Bible study part just wasn't worth being there for.

We've all been there.

So they've decided they're not going to put themselves through that again. Which is where this book wants to make a difference.

3. What ingredients should a small group have?

There isn't one correct answer to that question: different contexts will dictate different solutions. But here are some suggestions.

After Peter's sermon on the Day of Pentecost the new Christians *devoted themselves to the apostles' teaching and to fellowship, to the breaking of bread and to prayer* (Acts 2:42).

There are different views about celebrating the Lord's Supper in a small group. But it's likely that all Christians will agree that three key ingredients of a small group are the Bible (the apostles' teaching), love (fellowship) and prayer.

You may want to add evangelism to the list. Or something else.

4. So why did I write this book?

I'm a passionate believer in small group Bible study. So here are my three reasons for writing the book.

a. The Bible should be the foundation of everything

Of course the Holy Spirit has all kinds of ways to speak to us. But I am convinced that more than any other way he uses the Bible.

So it seems to me to make sense that Bible study should be the foundation of every small group.

But please don't let the expression *Bible study* put you off: I am not talking about something academic and unrelated to real life. I just mean taking the Bible seriously together and expecting the Holy Spirit to speak to us.

The aim of small group Bible study is not intellectual satisfaction or theological abstraction: it's about *encountering God* in his word.

b. It's the part many small group leaders struggle with

Some small group leaders use bought material that has been prepared by someone else: sometimes this can be a bit impersonal.

And if they prepare their own Bible studies they're not really sure how to do it: no one has ever offered them any training.

And this doesn't just apply to the preparation. Most small group leaders have never received basic training in how to lead the conversation when their group is studying the Bible.

c. Most written training material is not practical

I have seen some training material for group Bible study that just consists of general principles. But that doesn't get you very far.

So *How to Lead Group Bible Study so that People Meet God* is unashamedly a how-to book. It is full of practical suggestions and practical advice.

5. So who is this book for?

How to Lead Group Bible Study so that People Meet God has been written for three groups of people.

First, it is for Christians who want to start leading group Bible study.

Second, it is for Christians who already lead group Bible study but who want to do the job better.

And, *third*, it is for group Bible study leaders who want to train others to do this too.

If you come into any of these three categories, this book is for you.

6. How should this book be used?

a. Individually or with others

As I have already explained, *How to Lead Group Bible Study so that People Meet God* is designed as a practical course.

You may want to work through it on your own. Or you might decide to do this with a friend. This friend may be at the same stage as you, as far as Bible study leading is concerned, or they may be more, or less, experienced.

So you decide.

But I want to encourage you to consider meeting up regularly with at least one other Christian as you work through this book.

b. Not just reading but also doing the homework

That word *homework* may have put you off already!

But it is important. If you just read this book it will be of little benefit to you. When we want to develop a skill, we need to practise.

If you flick through the book you will see white boxes and grey boxes. The white boxes are simply for reading, but the grey boxes are headed up *Something to do*.

I hope you will take time to work on the suggested tasks in the grey boxes – either alone or with others.

Let me prove to you how seriously I take this.

If you do decide to do the homework, you will want to see my own suggestions and answers. But I have deliberately not put these in an appendix.

If I were reading a book like this and the author's suggestions were in an appendix, I would probably not bother doing the homework; instead I would just turn to the back of the book.

I hope that putting my answers and suggestions on www.howtoleadgroupbiblestudy.org will make it less likely that you will go for the lazy option!

c. With lots of prayer

The danger with a how-to book about group Bible study is that you read it and think *I can do this now – I've worked through the book!*

This brings us to the issue of spiritual battle.

Unless we are trusting in the power of the Holy Spirit and asking God to change us and equip us, there is no point in reading the book at all.

I am praying that God will be at work in you as you ask him to equip you to lead group Bible study so that people meet God.

I hope you will continue to read.

My belief is that the following things are essential if we are to grow as Bible study group leaders: a model, a method and a mentor.

We will examine these in the three main parts of the book.

Enjoy!

Part One

A Model

We need to find a model.

Most learning doesn't happen in a vacuum. The best learning comes from watching someone doing something they are good at – and then copying them. So I remember as a sixteen-year-old watching my father wallpapering a room and then trying it myself. And it worked.

This is a biblical principle. Paul tells the Christians in Corinth *Follow my example, as I follow the example of Christ* (1 Cor 11:1). And there was something similar happening with Jesus and his Father during the three years of his public ministry: *Very truly I tell you, the Son can do nothing by himself; he can do only what he sees his Father doing, because whatever the Father does the Son also does* (Jn 5:19).

1. Our need

So, when it comes to leading group Bible study, we need to find a model. Maybe a couple of people come to mind who you think lead group Bible study really well.

One of them may be someone who is in the same small group as you; the other may be someone who you remember from years ago: when they were leading, it was easy to talk and the Bible came alive.

But don't look for a model who seems to know the answer to pretty much every question anyone could ever ask; or who speaks in incredibly long paragraphs; or who constantly comes up with new explanations for Bible passages which no one else has thought of in 2,000 years of church history.

Instead, look for someone who loves God, who handles the Bible responsibly and enthusiastically, and who helps the group they're leading to find out what the passage means and to work out what that's going to mean for each of them in practice.

You may want to read that last paragraph again. Does anyone spring to mind?

2. My experience

Two of my models for group Bible study leadership are Christian Bensel and Gerhild Haitchi.

I met Christian when I was involved in mission work in Austria: for quite a few years I was a member of the small group he and his wife led in our church. One of Christian's qualities was the ability to help a group to be relaxed. None of us felt we were being tested; rather, his enthusiasm was infectious, so that we all *wanted* to get into the Bible and to get the Bible into us.

The result was that in our small group we weren't just encountering one another: we were encountering God too.

A second model for group Bible study leadership is Gerhild. When she was a student at her university in Austria, our Christian Union had the responsibility to prepare group Bible study materials for a national conference. I gave five students a passage each, and wondered what the result would be. With four of the students I needed to work with them on what they had produced, in order for it to become material worth using.

But when I read what Gerhild had prepared I remember thinking *Well, she's done a better job than I could have done!* The questions Gerhild had written were simple and clear: this was the ideal group Bible study outline. I don't think I had any suggestions for improvement.

Gerhild and her husband are now part of the same church as me in the UK, and she and I have sometimes produced Bible study materials together for our small groups. So the whole church family benefits from her gifts in preparing questions; and if reputation is anything to go by, she's great at actually leading a study too.

3. Your search

If you cannot think of a model group Bible study leader, it is time to pray and ask God for his help. If you need to, ask if you can visit other small groups to see some leaders in action (but maybe don't tell them why you want to come!).

But I suspect that most of you who are reading this don't have to look for a model group Bible study leader. You are already thinking of someone – someone God uses to help a small group encounter God in the Bible, so that a supernatural event takes place.

Something to do (1)

1. If nobody springs to mind who is a model group Bible study leader for you, ask God to bring you into contact with someone whose example will help you to grow as a group Bible study leader yourself.

2. But if you can think of one or two Bible study group leader models, thank God for them. And thank God for what he has done in your life through them.

3. What do you particularly appreciate about the way they lead group Bible study? Ask God to build those qualities into your life – and into your own group Bible study leading.

Go to www.howtoleadgroupbiblestudy.org for a few comments from me.

Part Two

A Method

Some books about leading group Bible study resist teaching a method. Instead they confine themselves to passing on basic principles: make sure you are faithful to the Bible passage, it is important to be clear, lead the discussion well.

But for most of us this isn't enough.

Suppose you can't swim and you ask me to teach you. I *could* decide to teach you basic principles: don't breathe under water, wave your arms and legs around, stay away from the deep end.

But that won't get you very far. What needs to happen is that I teach you a method of swimming, by which I mean a number of steps you can follow. Now of course, once you have started swimming you may find that you are going to do some things differently from the way I taught them to you in my method. That's fine. But a method is essential if you want to get started.

It's the same with leading group Bible study.

A method is not only essential, it must also be simple. Think of swimming again. Once you have learnt to swim there are lots of refinements and techniques you can incorporate into your style. But put those refinements and techniques into the basic method and you freak people out. The basic method needs to be just that: basic.

It is the same with group Bible study leading.

So the method I am teaching in this book consists of two basic steps: *Prepare well* and *Lead wisely*. *Prepare well* is about producing materials beforehand, while *Lead wisely* is about learning to lead the group discussion skilfully.

Of course that doesn't mean that all this is easy: sometimes, even after many years of leading group Bible study, I get stuck in my preparation or just lead the study badly. We never stop learning, which is why Part Three of this book is so important.

I hope you will try these two steps.

Step One: Prepare well

This is where we must start. It is obvious but so important that it is worth spelling out: you can't lead a group Bible study well if you haven't prepared well beforehand.

Preparing involves a number of things. But let's not forget: the foundation of it all is prayer. I want to do all my group Bible study preparation trusting in the God who gave us the Bible.

1. Find your Bible passage

This is no problem if all your small groups do the same series of studies, which are prepared in advance for you. So the materials simply arrive in your in-box: it's a series on Romans, or Jesus' parables.

> Sometimes using pre-prepared material gets the leader thinking *Oh good, I don't need to prepare!*
>
> Big mistake.
>
> For some advice if you are using pre-prepared materials, see point 8 on pages 29-30.

But if each small group is to choose what they will study, then you have a decision to make. You might want to give your group a few suggestions so you can decide together what to go for.

Unless everyone in your group is already very used to doing Bible study together, I suggest you leave more difficult Bible books till later: for example, Revelation, Joel, Ezekiel, Lamentations and Hebrews.

Instead, go for books (or parts of books) that will be more accessible because studying them demands less background knowledge: for example, the Sermon on the Mount (Matthew chapters 5-7), Philippians, a selection of Psalms, Mark and 1 Peter.

I don't recommend that you try to do a series in the whole of Romans or the whole of John's Gospel: the danger is that such series are too long. If you want to study John, then why not tackle chapters 1-12, then take a break and study something else, and then come back at a later stage to look at chapters 13-21?

It is for your group to decide how long each passage is going to be. In this book I'm going to focus on short passages; if you go for longer passages, then be aware of the fact that you are not going to be able to study in as much detail.

I am going to show you how I prepared a group Bible study on Philippians 1:1-11, and then ask you to try the same thing with another passage. But let me first stress that as I prepare I am asking the Holy Spirit to give me wisdom and creativity.

1 Paul and Timothy, servants of Christ Jesus, to all God's holy people in
Christ Jesus in Philippi, together with the overseers and deacons:
2 Grace and peace to you from God our Father and the Lord Jesus Christ.
3 I thank my God every time I remember you.
4 In all my prayers for all of you, I always pray with joy
5 because of your partnership in the gospel from the first day until now,
6 being confident of this, that he who began a good work in you will carry
it on to completion until the day of Christ Jesus.
7 It is right for me to feel this way about all of you, since I have you in my
heart and, whether I am in chains or defending and confirming the gospel,
all of you share God's grace with me.
8 God can testify how I long for all of you with the affection of Christ Jesus.
9 And this is my prayer: that your love may abound more and more in
knowledge and depth of insight,
10 so that you may be able to discern what is best and may be pure and
blameless for the day of Christ,
11 filled with the fruit of righteousness that comes through Jesus Christ –
to the glory and praise of God.

Philippians 1:1-11

2. Study the passage yourself

It's obvious: you can't prepare good materials for the Bible study unless you know what the passage is about.

My advice is that you don't immediately grab a commentary, although of course you might refer to one at a later stage (assuming you have such a thing).

There are all kinds of ways you can study a Bible passage (for example, with the four questions I outline in my book *How to Teach the Bible so that People Meet God*, pages 17-25).

But a simpler approach if you are preparing to lead a group Bible study is to try a slight adaptation of the Swedish method (which, I assume, was created in Sweden). This involves using a number of symbols to help you get into the passage. You grab a sheet of paper or a notebook and put the symbols down the left-hand side of the page. Here they are, with their meaning:

↑ *What is there in the passage about God or Jesus?*
↓ *What is there here about people?*
? *What is there here that I don't understand?*
! *If I was reading this for the first time, what would surprise me?*
💡 *Is there something I'm understanding for the first time?*
→ *How am I going to be different as a result of reading this?*

So this is what I ended up with after studying Philippians 1:1-11 using the Swedish method:

↑ God has a people who belong to him (1)
he's their Father and can give them grace and peace (2)
When people become Christians it's God who starts the whole process (6); he'll finish it too! (6)
God answers our prayers for one another (9-11)

↓P (this is about the apostle Paul)
he serves Jesus (1)
he prays for the church in Philippi (2, 4, 9-11)
he thanks God for them too, every time he thinks of them (3)
he tells them *why* he's grateful for them (5)
he's sure God is looking after these Christians and will bring them safely to the end of history (6)
he loves them very much (7-8)

↓C (this is about the church in Philippi)
they belong to God and have leaders (2)
they are enthusiastic about sharing the gospel (5)
they have experienced God's grace, just like Paul (7)

	they can expect great things to happen in their lives, as God answers Paul's prayers (9-11)
?	
!	v3 every time! v6 what confidence! v7 Paul's love!
💡	Paul doesn't just pray for them; he tells them *what* he's praying for them! (9-11)
→	I want to pray big prayers for others and tell them *what* I'm praying for them!

You may feel I have missed some important things: I can live with that.

You will have noticed that I adapted the symbols a little, because *one* arrow pointing down is not enough for this passage. We need *two* arrows pointing down: one for Paul (P) and one for the church in Philippi (C).

This will be true, one way or another, whenever you use the Swedish method.

Something to do (2)

Now that you have seen the process thus far with Philippians 1:1-11, please try it yourself with another passage: Mark 4:35-41. *It's a short passage, so you should get it done in around 10 minutes.*

Read the passage and ask God for his help. Then grab a piece of paper or a notebook and write the symbols on the left-hand side. I suggest you have one arrow pointing up, with a J beside it (for Jesus), and one arrow pointing down, with a d beside it (for the disciples). And then the other symbols as before.

When you have written down your answers next to the symbols, you can find my answers at www.howtoleadgroupbiblestudy.org.

3. Summarise the passage in one sentence

Some people call this the big idea.

The good thing about this is that it forces you to think about the passage as a whole rather than just as a collection of little bits.

I sometimes struggle with this, but it is absolutely worth doing.

You will decide for yourself whether you find this one-sentence summary *before* you study the passage, or *afterwards.* What is vital is *that* this gets done, not *when* it gets done.

So how am I going to summarise Philippians 1:1-11 in one sentence? Try this for size:

Paul shows his love for the church in Philippi by thanking God for them, encouraging them and praying for them.

I don't think my answer is stunningly good, but I think it'll do. You might come up with something better.

But the very fact that I try to find this summary will help me in my preparation.

Something to do (3)

Now please turn back to Mark 4:35-41. As you pray, write down a one-sentence summary of the passage. Please note: because this is a narrative, your summary will probably be of *what happens* in the passage.

When you have written down your suggestion, you can find my thoughts at www.howtoleadgroupbiblestudy.org.

4. Prepare suitable questions

The questions we prepare need to be of two kinds: observation questions and application questions. And all of them need to be *good* questions.

What follows will help us to understand why this is important and what it involves.

Q1. Why does this matter?

If we don't prepare questions we will end up talking too much during the group Bible study itself. And the last thing you want in your small group is the leader giving everyone else sermonettes.

You might be thinking *Well, I can make up the questions at the time – I don't need to prepare them*. But if you try to do that, some of your questions will be just plain bad. I speak from experience.

Q2. What do I mean by *observation* and *application*?

Observation questions help the group to see what the passage says and to talk about what it means. They will help everyone to look closely at the passage and to discuss with one another what the meaning is.

Application questions help the group to talk about what the passage is going to mean in practice in their own lives.

There is a difference between meaning and application.

It's an important distinction.

Meaning is general principles; application is practical examples.

The meaning of a passage (or part of one) might be that we should pray more. If you say that in a group Bible study everyone will probably agree. An observation question will get you that far.

But what does this principle mean *in practice*? If we all agree that we should pray more, *what practical step is each of us going to take to make sure it happens?* That's what an application question will help us to talk about.

Observation questions and application questions

Here are three examples of observation and application questions. After each observation question I have put the expected answer in brackets.

(Obs) *How do we think Titus is feeling when Paul encourages him in verses 2 and 3? Can we make a list? (Answers: excited / grateful / surprised)*
(App) *What could we do to encourage another Christian in the next few days?*

(Obs) *What does the writer of this psalm want us to do when we're feeling down? (Answer: Put our hope in God)*
(App) *What's that going to look like in practice for us?*

(Obs) *Let's look at verses 14-18. What does Peter want us to do when people are against our faith? (Answer: Pray)*
(App) *What can we do this week so that we end up spending more time in prayer?*

I hope it's clear: a general principle (we should pray) only becomes application when we start talking about what this is going to mean in our own lives.

This doesn't mean that I ask observation questions and application questions alternately. I will usually ask more observation questions than application questions; but application questions are *essential*.

So we need to prepare observation questions and application questions. That doesn't mean that in the study itself we will ask the application questions only after we have asked all the observation questions; but in general of course observation comes before application.

Q3. What do I mean by *good* and *bad* questions?

A good question is one that helps the group to look and see what the passage says and means (observation), or to talk about what it's going to mean for them in practice (application).

A bad question makes it much less likely that the group will talk in a relaxed way and be honest and open with each other. Some bad questions just result in silence or confusion.

Here are some examples.

A bad question

+ sounds like this is an exam:
Identify the three main reasons Jesus is opposed by the Pharisees and put that in the context of the Old Testament background.

+ is condescending:
I think it's very easy to see why Simon Peter says this. Can any of you see the reason?

+ has a Yes or No answer:
Isn't verse 6 wonderful?

+ is too long and complicated:
Why did the disciples, having already seen Jesus heal the sick woman and raise Jairus' daughter, fail to understand what Jesus wanted them to believe in chapters 3, 5 and 10?

+ is too easy:
In this incident Jesus turned water into wine. Where did this wedding take place?

Probably any of those bad questions will stop the conversation and create an awkward atmosphere. So what are some of the characteristics of good questions?

A good question

+ is easy to understand:
In verses 6-9, why does Peter say we should live our lives for God and his glory?

+ uses *we* rather than *you*:
In what sorts of ways do we make that kind of mistake?

+ uses the present tense:
Why does Jesus decide to heal the leper?
What reason does Peter give for writing his letter?

+ helps everyone dig deeper into the passage
Can we find any other reasons for what Paul says?

+ asks people for their opinion:
Why do we think the shepherds start telling everyone about Jesus?

+ includes *feeling*:
How do we think the woman feels when Jesus asks 'Who touched me?'

Using the present tense makes everything more immediate and easier to relate to. Asking about what someone in the story might have *felt* helps everyone to think their way into the situation.

And using *we* instead of *you* turns a teacher-and-pupils relationship into a friends-talking-together relationship. The atmosphere will be more relaxed; people will talk more freely.

Obviously not everything is a matter of opinion. But where you *can* ask for people's opinion on something, that takes away the fear of *giving the wrong answer.* So, when possible, *Why do we think..?* is a good way to go.

And if a good question is nevertheless a bit long, there's a simple solution: start with a statement, and *then* ask the question.

Something to do (4)

Please have a look at these questions, and decide which are good and which are bad. And, each time, *explain the reason for your decision*. Enjoy!

Q. Why do we think the disciples still don't recognise who Jesus is?
Q. Why do we think the Pharisees are so against Jesus?
Q. Extrapolate from this passage for your own lives.
Q. Who heals the woman in verse 29?
Q. Do any of you know where Paul says something similar in one of his letters?
Q. How do we think the Christians in Ephesus might have felt when this letter was read out?

When you have written down your answers you can find mine at www.howtoleadgroupbiblestudy.org.

5. Perhaps prepare a starter question

A starter question is a question at the very beginning of the study. It isn't directly related to the passage the group are going to be looking at, but it probably has something to do with one of the passage's main themes.

Some people call it an ice-breaker: if it involves people talking about their own experience, or if there is a funny side to it, the ice-breaker relaxes the group.

This is even more the case if you suggest people chat about the question in pairs. Even the most shy will often be willing to talk if they are just speaking to one other person.

One more thing needs to be said here. Obviously the starter question is the first one I'm going to ask. But when I write questions for a group Bible study, the starter question is normally the last one I prepare: I prepare everything else first.

6. My questions for a study on Philippians 1:1-11

Below are some of the questions I prepared for this Bible study. After a starter question these questions focus on verses 3-6: in other words I am not giving you my questions for the rest of the passage. I have included two observation questions and two application questions (See the O or the A after each question).

- Starter question: Can we talk in pairs about this? Can we think of a situation – maybe when we were at school – when we became aware that someone didn't care about us? What was it that they did or didn't do that showed that they didn't like us? (2 minutes)
- (Share in the whole group / read the passage / pray)
- [then there will be a couple of questions about verses 1 and 2]
- Now let's look at verses 3-6. What is there here that shows the Christians in Philippi that Paul loves them? (O)
- Paul thanks God for the church in verse 3. But why do we think he *tell*s them that he does this? (How do we think this makes them feel?) (O)
- Would we be embarrassed to say this kind of thing to one another? Why? (A)
- What could each of us do in the next few days to follow Paul's example here? (A)

I don't think these questions are brilliant. But let me say a couple of things about them:

+ I'm not sure that the first application question is really an application question at all, though it's nudging in that direction. Although it has a Yes or No answer, the *Why?* question after it makes that OK.

+ You will notice that the second observation question and the first application question actually consist of two questions. I won't ask both of those questions immediately: I will ask the first and see where the conversation goes; and use the second if I need it.

Something to do (5)

Turn back to Mark 4:35-41.

As you ask God to help you, please do the following:
write two observation questions;
write two application questions;
and then write a starter question.

> You will find it helpful to look back at the characteristics of good questions and bad questions on pages 24-25.
>
> When you have written down your answers, you can find my comments at www.howtoleadgroupbiblestudy.org.

I hope you have enjoyed working on *Step One: Prepare well.* If you don't have a go at preparing good observation and good application questions, you will never discover the massive impact this can have on a group Bible study.

And remember: preparing your questions with a friend, or running them past a friend after you've prepared them, will make it more likely that they are worth using. (For more on this, see point 3b on page 50.)

And will make it more likely that the group will meet God.

As we approach the end of *Step One*, there are a few more things worth mentioning.

7. Make sure your notes are clear

a. perhaps divided into sections

With a passage like Philippians 1:1-11, I will have the questions related to verses 1 and 2 together in my notes. When we're done with these I will say *OK, let's move on to verses 3-8*: so my questions on those verses will be together.

When we're done with those, I'll say *So now let's look at Paul's prayer in verses 9-11* and move on to those questions.

I hope that makes sense: I want to be able to find my way around my notes easily.

Of course in a short passage like Mark 4:35-41 I won't need to divide it into sections at all.

If the passage is very long I will not only divide it into sections: I will also not have the whole thing read out at the start. For example, if our passage is as long as Philippians 1:1-26 and we read the whole passage out at the beginning of the study time, most people will forget much of what we've read.

So I will say *OK, let's read verses 1-11*, and then we'll study those verses. Next I will say *Now let's read verses 12-18*: we then study that section of the chapter. And so on with verses 18b-26.

b. with some extra questions in brackets

When I write out my notes I will sometimes have another question or prompt, in brackets, after my main question. I will use the bracketed stuff only if I need it.

Let me give you an example.

One of my observation questions for the Philippians 1:1-11 study is *Now let's look at verses 3-6. What is there here that shows the Christians in Philippi that Paul loves them?*

It may be that the group come up with answers like *He thanks God for them, He prays for them, He's thrilled that they share his passion for evangelism* and *He's sure that God is going to look after them all the way to glory.*

But most groups won't get this far.

So I'll have a few additions in brackets, with prompts such as *There's another one in verse 3 I think*, or *Is there something in verse 5 too?* Obviously I'll only use these if I need them.

Of course, as I get more experienced in leading group Bible study, I won't need to write down these extra questions or prompts: it will become second nature to add such comments.

But my notes need to be clear.

8. How to use materials prepared by someone else

If you have been provided with notes for a series of group Bible studies, that saves you some work. But there are dangers.

If you are using pre-prepared material I hope you will still do the following things outlined above:

2. Study the passage yourself (see page 19)
3. Summarise the passage in one sentence (see page 21)

There are two other things which definitely need doing.

a. Decide if everyone is going to have the material

Personally I don't think it's great if everyone has the questions: it seems to me that the whole thing can begin to feel like a seminar rather than friends having a conversation.

And if you decide to miss out some questions, either because you don't like them or for time reasons, everyone will read the missing question and wonder why they're not getting to talk about it!

But you may decide that it's better if everyone has the materials.

It's your call.

b. Tidy up the questions

Don't assume that pre-prepared material is all going to be wonderful. So have a look at all the questions in advance and make changes as necessary.

So make sure there are observation questions and application questions.

And use the white boxes on pages 24 and 25 to help turn bad questions into good ones; delete questions you find unnecessary or unhelpful; and add new questions if they occur to you.

My impression is that most pre-prepared material is too long, so will need shortening: you will make your own decision. (I make some suggestions about how long a group Bible study should last on page 55.)

If we are going to lead a group Bible study we need to prepare well: this is Step One. Here is a reminder of the key things we have looked at:

Step One: Prepare well

1. Find your Bible passage

2. Study the passage yourself

3. Summarise the passage in one sentence

4. Prepare suitable questions (observation and application)

5. Perhaps prepare a starter question

6. Write clear notes for yourself

If you want to see my notes for a group Bible study of Philippians 1:1-11 and Mark 4:35-41, go to www.howtoleadgroupbiblestudy.org.

Before we move on to Step Two, there is something else to say about this first step.

Although Step Two is important, Step One is even more important. If we have not studied the passage ourselves and prepared suitable questions, it's hard to imagine how we will be able to lead a group Bible study in which people can meet God.

That is why Step One needs prayer and practice.

Step One: Prepare well

Step Two: Lead wisely

I'm aware that there are other ingredients in your small group meeting apart from Bible study. But in this book it's the Bible study part we're focusing on.

Most of what we will look at involves the actual leading of the study itself. But there are some important things to think about before it and after it, too.

1. Before the study

a. Prepare well

We have already looked at this: it is Step One of our method. Hopefully your notes have good observation and good application questions.

b. Pray

It makes sense to pray for myself as leader: that I will lead wisely, stay open to the Holy Spirit and be an example of someone wanting to meet God in his word.

I will pray, too, for every individual who may come to the meeting: that God will prepare them and give them exactly what they need.

And I pray for the group as a whole: that people will relate well to each other and be ready to learn from each other and from God. *My ultimate prayer goal is that everyone will meet God.*

c. Put the chairs in a circle

This is about ensuring that everyone in the group can see everyone else: that will make it much more likely that people will be able to talk in a relaxed way together.

I remember once attending a student group Bible study in a hall of residence. Four students were sitting along the side of the bed; one was sitting at the end of the bed, with his back to them; one was sitting on the floor between the wardrobe and the basin and could probably only see (and be seen by) half the group.

It didn't make for an open, relaxed conversation!

Obviously in some student rooms (and in some non-student rooms too) it's very hard to arrange the seating so that everyone can see everyone else.

But it is well worth the attempt.

And one more thing is worth adding. Normally I will reserve the seat I want to sit on, by leaving my Bible on it. If I don't do this, and if there's a good turnout this week, I may end up on a chair in an awkward position to lead from.

d. Create a relaxed atmosphere

Sometimes people arrive for a small group meeting stressed and tired. The atmosphere is awkward: it's like everyone's at the dentist's waiting for root canal work.

If things start like this, it's not a good foundation: people are unlikely to suddenly be able to start talking in a relaxed way about the Bible passage.

So what can we do?

It might be good to offer tea or coffee or juice as people arrive: holding a mug or a glass seems to put most people at ease. And maybe have some background music on.

There's something else too.

Sometimes everyone just sits pretty much in silence, or two people chat across the circle and everyone else is the audience.

You can change that in this way. Start up a conversation with the person to your right or your left: *How has your week been?* At first, others might start to listen in. But if the two of you are speaking fairly quietly, everyone else soon gets the message that audience status is not on offer here: they will all start to chat to their neighbours.

It works. Trust me.

And it creates a relaxed atmosphere.

Something to do (6)

Please take the opportunity to look back at the ideas of what you might do *before* the group Bible study:

Prepare well
Pray
Put the chairs in a circle
Create a relaxed atmosphere

Have a think about how these could work in the context of your own small group. You might even want to make a few notes. You can read mine at www.howtoleadgroupbiblestudy.org.

2. During the study

Three issues are worth considering.

a. How to start the study

Welcome the group, and suggest they all find the Bible passage you're going to be looking at together. You might need a couple of spare Bibles in case anyone has forgotten theirs.

The starter question

If I have a starter question (or ice-breaker) I will use that before an opening prayer. During Step One we saw how a starter question can help people to feel relaxed and to begin to think about one of the main themes of the Bible passage (see page 26).

My advice is not to spend too long on this. Two minutes is usually enough time for talking in pairs, followed by a few minutes for people who want to share what they've said with the whole group.

Reading the passage

I'm not a fan of reading around the group a verse at a time. Some people just don't want to read aloud in front of others; and everyone reading one verse means that sometimes there's a break in the middle of a sentence.

A better way is to say *OK, let's read the passage. If someone starts reading at verse 1, just read a few verses and stop where you like. Then someone else will read a few verses. And so on. Thanks. Someone start us off please.*

In my experience this is a much more natural way of reading the passage. And a group that meets regularly very soon gets used to this approach.

But you will do what works for your group.

An opening prayer

When I lead a group Bible study we never have a group prayer time at the beginning: my impression is that people are often too tired or stressed to want to join in. In my experience group prayer times are better *after* the Bible study than *before* it.

So usually I just pray a short prayer myself, or ask someone else to do it.

Here, then, is the normal order of events at the beginning of almost any group Bible study I lead:

- I ask the starter question and say *Let's talk about this in pairs.*
- After two minutes (anything longer is too long) I call everyone together and ask if anyone would like to share anything with us.
- We read the passage we are going to study.
- I pray that the Lord will speak to us.

Something to do (7)

You might want to review what we've just looked at about how to start the Bible study part of your small group meeting:

the starter question
reading the passage
an opening prayer

You might even want to take a few notes. You can read mine at www.howtoleadgroupbiblestudy.org.

b. What the leader should be like

Here are seven qualities that the leader of a group Bible study should ideally have; and it's helpful if the rest of the group have them too. But please don't think that being weak in any of these areas disqualifies you from being a leader: we're all on a learning curve.

After all, that's what disciples are: learners. So it's obvious where we should start.

i. a growing disciple. I want to be praying (see 1b on page 32), which comes naturally because I'm going to be a bit nervous. And I need to be open to the Holy Spirit, trusting that he will bless our Bible study and let us all meet God.

And an important part of being a Jesus disciple is that I'm going to love the others in my small group. They are not my enemies: they're my brothers and sisters.

And if *I'm* a growing disciple, others are going to want to be growing disciples too.

ii. enthusiastic. If the group think I seem a bit bored before we even start, that could be infectious. So I want to communicate that I am excited about what we are doing.

This is not about being artificially enthusiastic. You may be naturally quiet and reserved, but you can be enthusiastic in a way that fits your personality and style.

iii. encouraging. I want to make sure that I am looking around at the group as I ask a question, and also as people are contributing to the conversation. There's a danger that as soon as someone starts saying something, my head goes down to see what my next question is.

I can encourage whoever is speaking by looking at them, nodding, smiling, or whatever comes naturally to me. If all they see when they look at me is the top of my head or a blank stare, they are not getting the encouragement they need.

When I was a schoolteacher I led a Bible study group at a conference for students in their A-Level year. The conversation at our first meeting was stilted and awkward: whenever anyone said anything, the only person they saw actively encouraging them was me.

So after the study was over I took the opportunity to chat to everyone else in the group individually – over coffee, lunch or whatever. I asked them something like *What A-Levels are you doing?* When they started replying I just stared at them, or looked around the room.

It didn't take long before they said *What's wrong?* I replied *Nothing. Go on, and what do you hope to do next?* And then, as soon as they were talking again, I went back to just looking around or giving them the blank stare.

By this time they were laughing and asking what I was up to.

I said *I'm doing to you what we were all doing to one another in the Bible study*, and explained about the signals we all give off (smiling, nodding etc) when we're listening to someone talking.

Our group's second Bible study was wonderful: whenever anyone said something they could see the others actively encouraging them.

Eleven of the twelve group-members contributed, and the twelfth looked like he was about to at one point, before remembering *Hang on, I'm the one who never says anything in a Bible study.*

But in our third Bible study he was talking too.

Here's another thought about encouragement. There is a danger that the person answering one of the questions only looks at me, because it was me that asked it.

I can nearly always sort that in this way. If Nicki is only looking at me as she is talking, I will quickly glance round the rest of the group. Almost without realising that she's doing it, Nicki, still speaking, will look around at everyone else – and hopefully see a group of people offering their own silent encouragement as they listen.

Of course my encouragement can also be verbal. When someone contributes I need to be ready to say *Thank you,* or *Wow, that's great.*

This is the power of encouragement: it makes a massive difference. As leaders we can be encouraging, and we might want to encourage our group to be encouraging too.

iv. watchful. If I'm watching I sometimes see someone who was obviously about to say something but was beaten to it by someone else. After hearing what that someone else has to offer, I may then say *Did you want to say something about that, Claire?*

It could be the prompt that she needs.

If I'm watching I may sometimes notice someone's silent but emotional response to something that has been said. We're talking about relating to our parents, and maybe Joe never knew his parents or his relationship with his father was abusive as he was growing up.

I'm not going to force Joe to talk about this publicly, of course. But if I notice this is an area of hurt for him I may decide to move on to the next part of the passage more quickly than I had originally planned (see point v, below).

And I may think it right to chat to Joe one-to-one afterwards to see if talking about this would help him (see point b on page 45).

But if I'm not watching I will never see these things.

v. flexible. In front of me I have my observation and application questions. The danger is that I follow my notes slavishly, when sometimes I maybe should do a detour.

For example, someone says something that isn't what I had expected but is still relevant to the passage. Do I simply plough on regardless with my next prepared question? Or do I encourage a conversation about what's just been said?

I don't think there is a right answer here: it depends on the situation. But I need to be flexible and open to the Spirit, and not unnecessarily tied to my notes.

I will need this flexibility, too, if I am keeping my eye on the time. If the study is in danger of taking too long, I will need to miss out some questions.

(For some suggestions about how long the Bible study part of a small group meeting might last, see page 55.)

vi. inclusive. Because I am the leader I am asking nearly all the questions. There is a danger that the study looks like this: I ask a question, Phil replies; I ask another question and Sarah replies; I ask a third question and Alice replies.

In other words, every second person who speaks is me. Which is much closer to the teacher-and-students model than to the friends-talking-together model: it's more like a seminar than a conversation.

The solution is to leave room for others to respond to what Phil has said. When he's done, I might say *What do the rest of us think?* or *Do we agree with that?* or *Do we think Phil's right?* or *Does anyone want to add to what Phil's said?*

So in this way I'm deliberately including others and so avoiding the me-Phil-me-Sarah-me-Alice pattern.

Another way of getting more people included in the conversation is to ask a question and then say *Let's talk about this in pairs*. I often add *If you can't think of anything to say, talk about the weather and I'll think you're talking about my question*. But that's just *my* way of helping people to not feel under pressure.

After people have talked in pairs it is going to be much easier to include more people in the conversation: *Would anyone like to share what they've come up with?*

It's all part of being inclusive: helping as many people as possible to be involved in the discussion.

One other thing about including others. If someone in the group asks a question, they may well only be looking at me, because I'm leading the study this week. If I think I know the answer it's very tempting just to give it; but it's much better if I say *That's a great question. What do we think?*

vii. honest. Some people who are starting to lead group Bible study have the feeling that they need to know the answer to every question and to understand everything in the passage. We don't.

It isn't OK to be honest, it's *essential*: if we are not being real, how can we expect anyone else to be?

So it's fine to say *I have no idea what Paul means in verse 6! Can anyone help me?* And it's healthy to tell the group *I sometimes find myself giving up praying, but maybe this story is going to help me to keep going.*

Honesty isn't just the *best* policy. It's *biblical*.

Something to do (8)

Why not take some time to think and pray about the characteristics of a good group Bible study leader? There is no one who perfectly possesses all these qualities, but the Holy Spirit wants to equip us so that we can help others.

As you review the list, you might want to do three things: first, see if you want to change it at all; second, write down the qualities where you feel you need the most help from the Holy Spirit; and third, pray especially about these things, perhaps with a good friend.

Here is a reminder of the list. A group Bible study leader should be
a growing disciple
enthusiastic
encouraging
watchful
flexible
inclusive
honest

You can find a few more comments from me at www.howtoleadgroupbiblestudy.org.

c. Dealing with the problems

Whenever I lead a group Bible study, problems occur.

It's different when I'm preaching a Bible passage. Provided I've prepared properly I can preach, and there usually aren't any interruptions or unexpected events. Even if I feel like I'm doing a really bad job, I can just plough on and finish what I started.

But because group Bible study is much more of an interactive event, things will happen that I wasn't reckoning with.

It's one of the things that make group Bible study leadership exciting. And scary.

Here are some of the many things that may happen.

i. Mia loves tangents: she will say something that has nothing to do with what the group are discussing at the moment.

It might be right to say *Mia, can we come back to that in a minute?* if her comment is relevant to the passage. But sometimes I'll ask *Sorry Mia, what verse is that connected to?*

ii. Liam has a favourite subject: it's the second coming of Jesus, or intercessory prayer. They're both important, but they're not always relevant. So he drags his favourite topic into the conversation at the most unexpected times, sometimes with considerable ingenuity.

So I'll say *Sorry Liam, where's that in the passage?* Usually that's enough. But we all have favourite subjects and find them very difficult to let go of, so if Liam persists, I may need to have a chat with him afterwards along the lines of *Obviously the second coming of Jesus is incredibly important, but can you help us all to stick to the passage more?*

iii. Charlotte almost never speaks: she's very shy. The last thing I want to do is to force her to say something: she might just decide that this is the last time she's going to come to our small group.

But most people like Charlotte can cope with talking with one other person. So I will often ask a question and then say *Let's talk about this in pairs.* After a couple of minutes I interrupt everyone and ask *Does anyone want to tell us what they came up with?*

Charlotte doesn't need to respond to that of course. But it's fascinating: sometimes, having heard her own voice as she was talking to the other person in her pair, she will happily say something.

Especially if the rest of the group are sending her encouraging signals (see point iii on page 36).

iv. Will is always the first to speak, whenever I ask a question: he's a quick thinker and would never think of holding back. And this becomes a pattern: after a time the rest of the group instinctively hold back themselves so that Will can answer every question.

If he's done it a few times in a row (the study is in danger of becoming a conversation between me and Will, with everyone else as the audience), I'll interrupt him as soon as he pitches in: *Hang on, Will: can we hear what other people think, and then come back to you?*

After one or two other people have contributed I make sure I remember my promise: *Do you agree with that Will, or did you want to say something else?*

But it may be that I need to talk to Will one-to-one. I'll tell him that it's great that he's in the group and that he has so much to offer the rest of us: *But I think it's really important that the two of us let others have their say. So is it OK if you're not always the first person to answer every question?*

v. Sophie is a Christian but she questions everything. So she might say *I can see that that's what the passage says, but who says this bit of the Bible is worth taking seriously?* Or *That's what they thought when Paul wrote this, but we know better now, don't we?*

This might throw the whole discussion off course. So, after seeing what others have to say, I would tell Sophie *Well, at the moment we're just looking to see what the passage says. Maybe another time we can talk about whether the Bible is really reliable and relevant. Is that OK, Sophie?*

Usually this enables the Bible study to stay on course. But maybe afterwards I can chat to Sophie one-to-one, and recommend a good book (or, even better, a chapter in a book) about why we can trust the Bible. If I have a copy of the book to lend her, that's even better.

It's important that Sophie knows that I take her questions seriously. But it's also important that I don't allow her doubts to derail the Bible study.

vi. Ben has a history with someone else in the group. Maybe it's a personality clash or one of them once made a comment that upset the other. But in any case, whenever Dan says something Ben is likely to rubbish it.

When this actually happens I might just say *What do other people think about what Dan said?* Or *Why do you think that, Ben?*

But I may well need to talk to Ben one-to-one and ask him straight out if he has a problem with Dan. Perhaps it'll even be necessary to get the two of them together to talk out their problem, either on their own or with me as a referee.

vii. Emma does her best to take over the leadership of the Bible study. So when I've asked a question she might say *But what we really need to be asking is why the church in Colosse has the problem in the first place.*

Now of course she might be right. Maybe I'll say *OK, thanks Emma, let's talk about that first.* But I might think it's better to say *We'll come back to that in a minute if that's OK, Emma. But for now let's talk about...* (and I'll ask my original question again).

As a basic principle: I have prepared to lead this group Bible study, so it's better if I lead it.

If I think it's necessary I'll talk to Emma afterwards one-to-one. And of course, without realising it she may be just waiting for the opportunity to be trained as a group Bible study leader herself (see point 3 on page 56 for more on this).

Something to do (9)

Unexpected things can throw us when we're leading a group Bible study: it happens to all of us. I can think of other surprise events which can easily derail things; perhaps you can too.

Please review the problems that we've just looked at together. You might want to make notes on the following: What other tricky issues have you seen crop up in a small group Bible study? What other solutions can you think of, apart from what I have suggested?

Mia goes off at a tangent
Liam and his favourite subject
Charlotte never speaks
Will always crashes in first
Sophie has fundamental doubts about basics
Ben has a personality clash with Dan
Emma is almost taking over leading the study

When you have made some notes, you can see some more comments from me at www.howtoleadgroupbiblestudy.org.

3. After the study

When the Bible study itself is over, my job as leader is not done.

a. Help the group to pray

It makes sense to pray together at the end of the Bible study: we want to ask God to help us build what we have learnt into our own lives. But very often the leader will say *Well, we're going to pray. But before we do, does anyone have anything they would like prayer for?*

So people share prayer needs and then the group prays.

What nearly always happens is that the personal prayer needs get prayed about: after all, they are fresh in everyone's memories because they've just been mentioned. *But hardly anyone prays about what the group has learnt from the Bible passage.*

And Satan is laughing.

So I suggest that it makes much more sense to have two times of prayer.

The first time of prayer

I say something like *Well, we're going to have two times of prayer. In the first we'll pray about the passage and in the second we'll pray for our own needs. So let's keep our Bibles open to remind us of what we've just read, and pray about what we've been talking about.*

The second time of prayer

I will close off the first time of prayer and then say *Well, does anyone have anything they'd like us to pray for?*

After people have shared I might add a couple of general prayer needs for the church or the CU or the world, and then I will lead us into the prayer time.

It is much better to have two times of prayer than to have one time of prayer in which the group don't pray about what we've learnt from the Bible passage.

How (not) to lead a prayer time

If I want prayer times full of awkward silences and with less than half the group praying out loud, here's how. I pray a first prayer that is impressive, maybe one that reminds God of the whole of Old Testament salvation history. Perhaps including sentences like *And then, Lord, there was Gideon*.

And, above all, I make sure my prayer is *long*. The longer the better.

Then this will happen: during my prayer, people who might otherwise have thought they would pray out loud are changing their minds. They're thinking *Wow, that's an amazing prayer Andrew's praying: I could never pray as well as that. I'll just keep quiet and pray in my heart.*

It's very common that Christians speaking the first prayer do just what I've described. It's a recipe for a lousy prayer time.

But there is another way.

As I lead us into the prayer time I often say *Let's pray short prayers*. Then I'll pray the first prayer: if I don't, someone else might pray a prayer like the one I described five paragraphs ago.

So I'll pray a one- or two-sentence prayer and say *Amen*. All round the group people are thinking *Oh wow, I could pray a prayer like that*.

And they do.

If praying together like this becomes a habit for your small group, more and more people will start praying aloud. This *works.*

There's something else. As I start a prayer time off I say *And I'll close the prayer time at the end.*

Imagine what happens if I *don't* say this.

After a few people have prayed, there's a silence when no one is praying. Instead of praying silently, some people are thinking *Maybe everyone else has stopped praying now and I'm the only one with my eyes still shut.*

So they put their hands over their faces, with their fingers slightly apart so they can see through the gaps: and they look to see if the prayer time has finished or not. I know this happens, because I've often done it myself.

That is such a waste. If I have said I'm going to close in prayer and I haven't done it yet, that means we're still praying. If no one wants to pray out loud at the moment, we can all pray silently. Which is fine.

I hope you understand what I'm getting at.

So when I lead a prayer time, I say that I'll pray the closing prayer, and make sure that I pray *short* prayers. And I will pray several times during the prayer time: if I don't, people get the message that once they've prayed once, their job is done.

And my closing prayer needs to be very obviously a closing prayer. Maybe something like *Father, thank you that you've heard all our prayers. We bring them all to you in the name of Jesus. Amen.*

Forgive me for labouring the point as I talk about prayer at the end of a group Bible study. But I think it's important.

And, as I said earlier, *it works*.

b. Be open for important conversations

There are two kinds of important conversations which might need to happen after the group Bible study.

Sometimes a group member will approach you and want to talk about something: maybe there's something that's upset them.

But sometimes it'll be you taking the initiative: you noticed during the study that someone went really quiet and withdrew emotionally when the conversation was about a particular topic.

In both cases I need to be ready and available.

If it's a woman needing help I might think it appropriate to link her up with one of the other women in the group. Sometimes I ask one of the women in the group if she would be willing to contact another female member of the group, just to check that she's OK.

And of course some people will get the help they need from someone who isn't in our small group at all. Sometimes we can put someone in touch with the right kind of helper.

So I need to be ready, available and sensitive. The important thing is that everyone in the group gets the message that they *matter*: we want to support each other through life's ups and downs.

c. After everyone has gone home

There are three things I need to do if I have led a small group Bible study.

First, I will ask a friend how I could have done the job better. Find someone who will tell you the positives and the negatives of how you led. (There is more about this in *Part Three: A Mentor*.)

Second, I will follow up anything that has struck me from the study we've just had (see point b above). Maybe it would be good if I just sent an encouraging text or email to someone, just to say thank-you. There is massive potential here to encourage others.

And *third*, I will pray for the whole group. I don't mean just a quick *Lord, please bless our small group.* Instead I will take time to pray for everyone individually. That might not be that same evening (I'm tired!), but it will certainly be in the next few days.

Something to do (10)

I suggest you make brief notes about things you might do after the study. Which of these three elements has struck you most? And what are the main things you want to try to put into practice?

a. Help the group to pray
b. Be open for important conversations
c. After everyone has gone home

Take a few minutes to pray through what you have jotted down.

When it comes to leading group Bible study we need a method that is simple. So this is what we have looked at:

Part Two: A Method

Step One: Prepare well
1. Find your Bible passage
2. Study the passage yourself
3. Summarise the passage in one sentence
4. Prepare suitable questions (observation and application)
5. Perhaps prepare a starter question
6. Write clear notes for yourself

Step Two: Lead wisely
1. How to start the study
2. What the leader should be like
3. Dealing with the problems

Of course you may decide to do some things differently from the way I outline here. But I hope you will at least give my suggestions a try.

We will not grow as group Bible study leaders if we don't try to learn from others and ask the Holy Spirit to equip us.

And let's not forget: the aim is that our small groups study the Bible *and meet God.*

Part Three

A Mentor

Nobody likes to get stuck.

But that's what will happen if we're not open to receiving advice as to how we can do something better.

I am fairly confident that I lead group Bible study better now than I did when I first started out (though I still find myself leading the occasional nightmare Bible study).

That's down to the Holy Spirit equipping me; it's down to practice and experience; and it's down to my asking people for help and correction.

I have never had someone who was my *group Bible study leadership mentor*, but I have always had people around me who have helped me to become a better group Bible study leader.

So I'm not urging you to find someone you're going to call your mentor in group Bible study, though that's not a bad idea. Feel free to do exactly that.

But I *am* suggesting that it makes sense to have one or two friends whose comments and advice we listen to. In what follows I'm referring to such people as *mentors*.

That is what Part Three is about.

1. Who could your mentor be?

It might be someone who is in the same small group as you.

They may lead group Bible study themselves, or they may not. But you notice that they are good at picking up things which could make your leading of group Bible study *better*.

Or it might be someone who isn't part of the same group as you at all. So although they don't actually *see* you leading a study, you sometimes show them the questions you've written down in preparation to lead.

2. What should a mentor be like?

Don't ask someone with the gift of discouragement! A mentor should be quick to encourage but also ready to tell the truth, even if that's sometimes uncomfortable for them and for you, too.

Make sure the person you ask *understands* group Bible study.

Don't take it for granted that all preachers do. There are some Bible teachers who, while being in favour of small groups, don't *get* group Bible study: put them in a small group and it isn't a conversation because they can't say one sentence without immediately tacking on five more.

But don't get me wrong. Of course there are preachers who *do* get group Bible study. I hope I'm one of them.

So look for a friend who understands that key ingredients of group Bible study are observation questions and application questions, who can spot the difference between good questions and bad questions, and who knows that the aim of group Bible study is that everyone meets God as the Holy Spirit uses his word in our lives.

You might want to read that last paragraph again. Does anyone spring to mind?

3. How can your mentor help you grow?

There are a number of ways. Here are three.

a. by helping you prepare

It can be a huge help to prepare with someone else.

Maybe you do all the preparation for one Bible study together. Or sometimes you prepare on your own but show your notes to your mentor for their comments, so you can make any necessary changes before the group meets.

Or if you get stuck in your preparation because you just don't understand what verses 15 and 16 mean, you have someone you can ask for help.

b. by giving you feedback

If your mentor is part of the same small group as you, this feedback will be about your questions and also about how you led.

But if they are not in the same group as you their comments will just be about your questions. (Of course you can ask someone else who *was* there for their comments on how you led.)

And it will always be a help to have someone to talk to after the study, especially if you have the feeling that it was not your finest hour.

c. by praying for and with you

It's true: it's an amazing thing to know that someone is praying for us.

And sometimes you could meet up with your mentor to pray for your group Bible study leading, and to pray together for the members of your small group.

There are times when leadership of any kind can be a lonely experience. Having a friend who's praying *for* you and who can pray *with* you can make a massive difference.

Something to do (11)

Whether or not you use the word *mentor*, you may already have someone who fulfils the role we've just been looking at.

But if not, take a few minutes to think and pray about these issues:

1. Can you think of someone who's an encourager *and* who gets group Bible study? They may be a member of the small group you're part of, or they may not be.
2. Could you imagine asking them to fulfil the role of a mentor for you in your group Bible study leading (whether you use the word *mentor* or not)?
3. If you can't think of anyone who might be this person for you, take time to ask God for his direction. He answers prayers like this.

You can read a few more comments from me on this at www.howtolead groupbiblestudy.org.

Conclusion

How to Help People Meet God

There is power in the word of God. Which is just one reason why it makes sense for small groups to have the Bible as their foundation.

Group Bible study is not only an opportunity to receive information. It's about encounter. Not just encounter with one another – though that's obviously very important – but encounter with God.

If you have ever had the experience of knowing that God was speaking to you through the Bible, then you long for others to hear God too.

Which is why I have written *How to Lead Group Bible Study so that People Meet God.*

Thank you for taking the time to read and to work through the book. Whether you are already an experienced group Bible study leader, just starting out, or somewhere in between, I hope there have been things here which have stimulated you to grow.

Just writing this book has brought me a new excitement about leading group Bible study myself.

If I love the small group I'm a part of I'm going to want to pray for everyone.

Not just for their immediate needs: one person looking for a job, another struggling with loneliness, another coping with bereavement.

I also want to be praying that everyone in the group will grow in their knowledge of the God they've come to know though trusting in Jesus.

That's a great prayer to pray.

Or I can borrow some of the Bible's prayers and pray it for our small group and every individual in it. Maybe you'd like to pray this prayer now for the group you're part of:

And this is my prayer: that your love may abound more and more in knowledge and depth of insight, so that you may be able to discern what is best and may be pure and blameless for the day of Christ, filled with the fruit of righteousness that comes through Jesus Christ – to the glory and praise of God.
Philippians 1:9-11

Thank you for your willingness to help your small group meet God in his word. It's a huge responsibility to take on, and a huge honour too.

And the Holy Spirit loves to equip the children of God.

It's an awesome thought: as we lead group Bible study that same Spirit may choose to make this a supernatural event.

Doesn't that make you want to pray?

Something to do (12)

1. Run through the whole of this book in your mind, thinking especially about the following:
   A Model
   A Method
   Prepare well
   Lead wisely
   A Mentor
2. Write a list of 3, 4 or 5 things you want to do as a result of having worked through this book.
   And pray about them.

Appendix

Frequently Asked Questions

1. How long should a group Bible study be?

Of course there isn't one *right* answer to this. Your answer to the question will depend on the make-up of your group and on whatever other ingredients your small group meeting has.

I think the danger with some small groups is that the Bible study part is too long. This can result in the whole meeting finishing too late for some people: they may decide not to come back next week.

So in general I aim for the Bible study part to last around 45 minutes.

If you add to this general chat and sharing, and prayer about the passage and for each other's needs, this might bring you to a meeting of around 90 minutes.

I think it's worth deciding when you plan to finish the meeting by, and then working out a rough timetable on the basis of that.

2. How can I lead group Bible study online?

This has become an important question with the pandemic of 2020/2021 and its various lockdown restrictions.

I have been surprised how well this has gone for the home group I'm a part of. Here is my main thought: you might dismiss this as irrelevant to your group, and adapt it for your situation.

It may just be my age (I am 68 as I write this), but I find life on Zoom quite tiring. And I think I'm not the only one.

Which means we have made the following decision.

We have reduced the length of our weekly meeting so that it is closer to 60 minutes than 90 minutes. Here is what the schedule normally looks like:

a. Brief welcome and chat as people arrive (5 minutes)
b. Bible study (25 minutes)

Unusually we ask everyone to have read the passage before they arrive: this saves us time.

c. Prayer together about the passage we've just studied (10 minutes)

d. Sharing about personal needs and prayer together (20 minutes)

One other thing is worth sharing, but which may not be appropriate in your group. When we want to contribute, some of us are a bit slower to start speaking than others: the danger is that they never get the chance to speak at all, because someone else has already started.

So we have introduced a system where people wave if they want to speak or pray: when I see them I will say their name. We do the same in our prayer times, too.

This way no one feels excluded.

In practice our meetings online have lasted between 55 and 65 minutes. I think that for most of us that has been long enough. And of course this is supplemented by contact with each other in some way during the week.

These are reflections on the small group I am part of. But of course yours may be very different from mine.

3. How can I train others to lead group Bible study?

You may already be doing this.

If you want to train someone who is in the same small group as you are, then here is one possibility. Ask them if they would like to prepare the group Bible study *with you* in a few weeks' time.

You do the preparation together, and in that way they learn about observation questions and application questions, and about the difference between good questions and bad questions.

Then maybe *you* lead the Bible study.

But next time, do it the other way around. The two of you prepare everything together, but *they* lead the actual study. You are there as a support during the meeting, and you can talk together afterwards about what went well and what went less well.

Normally I wouldn't recommend two people actually leading a group Bible study together. I think that can get a bit confusing.

If you are wanting to train more people in leading group Bible study, you could offer two training sessions in your church or CU. There could be an open invitation for anyone who's interested, but you could also target people who you would particularly like to be there.

The first session is called *Prepare well* and the second is called *Lead wisely*. Those titles probably sound familiar!

My suggestion is that those who want to take this further could be given this opportunity when they are going to lead a group Bible study for the first time: *they could prepare with someone else* who maybe has more experience, and have that person in the study itself, ready to help them out if they get stuck.

And another thing (no surprise here!): You could give anyone you're training a copy of *How to Lead Group Bible Study so that People Meet God*.

4. How can I do Bible study one-to-one?

If I am going to do one-to-one Bible study I don't prepare observation and application questions as I do when I am going to lead a group.

That would immediately put us in a teacher-and-student scenario, which I don't think is helpful.

I react similarly to the idea of using pre-prepared materials designed for one-to-one Bible study. To me that is going to feel academic, as if my friend and I are answering exam questions together.

An exception to this is the *Uncover Mark* material produced by UCCF and IFES. Check it out: it's outstanding.

So when I do one-to-one Bible study I don't prepare any questions. I don't go through the whole of *Step One: Prepare well,* though I will certainly have read the passage through and prayed for our meeting.

A method of one-to-one Bible study

I ask Pete if he would like to study the Bible with me. At our first meeting I pray a short prayer that God will speak to us through the Bible passage we're going to look at today.

Then we read the passage. One of us does this, or (even better) we read it together in the way I outlined on page 34.

This is how I explain the method we're going to use.

Let's just ask one another questions. They can be a mixture of questions we know the answer to and questions we don't know the answer to. And the thing is: the more questions we ask, the fewer answers we have to come up with!

My experience is that this works. At first the other person is often a bit unsure, especially if they haven't done much Bible study before. So in our first session it might be me asking most of the questions. But I will leave gaps so there is time for him to ask something too if he wants to.

I will deliberately be asking good questions (see the box on page 24) such as *How do we think the leper might be feeling when Jesus says this?*

And I will include questions which I clearly don't know the answer to: *I haven't a clue what verse 14 is all about. Have you any idea?*

The advantage of a question like that is that it makes clear to my friend that this is not a teacher-and-student scenario, even if I have been a Christian longer than he has. It puts us on the same level: we are both learners, both wanting to know more about what it means to follow Jesus.

And the advantage of the whole method is that Pete gets used to the idea of *asking questions of a Bible passage*. Think about it: this is actually the key to all Bible study, whether you are with others or on your own.

Then at the end of our study, which will be no longer than 45 minutes, we pray together. We do that in a similar way to what I described on pages 43-45.

But this time I call it table-tennis praying: it's short prayers, to and fro. But I make it clear to Pete that he doesn't have to pray aloud: we can both use the gaps between my prayers to pray silently if he feels more comfortable with that.

If we both have our Bibles still open in front of us, and if I pray one- or two-sentence prayers, it's not long before Pete starts praying out loud too.

I encourage you to try this method of one-to-one Bible study.

A story about Herbert

A friend of mine in Austria became a Christian. I asked Herbert how he would feel about us studying John's Gospel together, and he was positive. I made it clear that he wasn't committing himself to us doing all twenty-one chapters: either of us could say at any point *This has been great, but I think it's time to stop.*

We used this method: we asked one another questions.

It took us a full year to get through the whole of John, meeting usually for an hour a week. It was wonderful.

Some years later Herbert joined the leadership team of his church and he's still following Jesus. This is the Holy Spirit using the Bible in someone's life.

A story about Christian

I did the same thing with Christian. He wanted to study Matthew's Gospel, which we did, over many months, just asking one another questions.

Four or five years later it was time for me to leave Austria and come home to the UK. Shortly before I left Christian and I were chatting about his journey with Jesus. I asked him *Of all the things you've done and experienced, what is it that God used most in your life to help you grow?*

When I asked that question I had no idea what he would say: I was just interested. Christian looked at me and said *Studying Matthew's Gospel with you.* He hadn't even needed time to think about it.

I was astonished. Don't get me wrong: I had enjoyed our weekly meetings to do the next half-chapter of Matthew. But I don't remember ever thinking when Christian had gone home *Wow that was amazing this week: the Holy Spirit is so at work here.*

And yet he clearly was. He was using his word to build Christian into the mature leader he is today, both in church work and in the student world.

As I look back on my twenty years in Austria I'd say that reading the Bible one-to-one with a friend (just asking one another questions) was one of the most important things I ever did there.

If you have never done this, maybe it's something you'd like to try?

Something to do (13)

Have a think about the four questions dealt with here. You might like to write down anything that has particularly struck you.

1. How long should a group Bible study be?
2. How can I lead group Bible study online?
3. How can I train others to lead group Bible study?
4. How can I do Bible study one to one?

Do you need to take action about any of these four areas? If so, it would be good to pray about this.

There are some comments from me at howtoleadgroupbiblestudy.org.

How to Teach the Bible so that People Meet God

Andrew Page

Andrew Page believes that Bible teaching can be a supernatural event. A graduate of London School of Theology, Andrew was a missionary in Austria for 20 years, working with the Austrian Christian student movement (IFES) and later pastoring a church in Innsbruck.

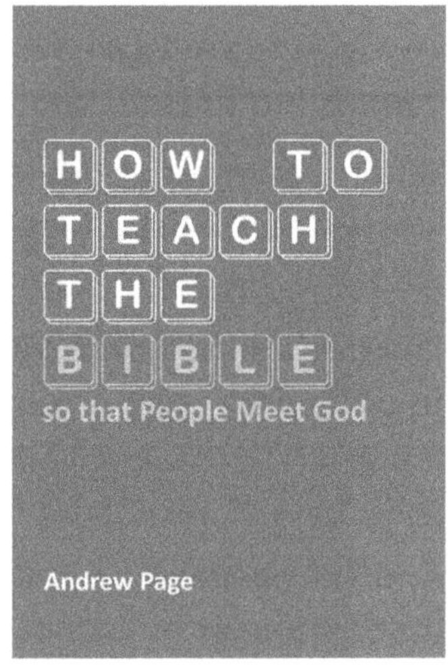

He says "Two enemies of Christian churches are Bible teaching with little biblical content and Bible teaching which is more a lecture than an event." If you agree with this, *How to Teach the Bible so that People Meet God* is the book for you.

This is unashamedly a how-to book. Andrew has trained others in this method of teaching a Bible passage in a number of countries around Europe, and now for the first time the method is available as a book.

So, 3 questions before you buy this book:
- Do you want to find out if God has given you the gift of teaching?
- Do you want to grow in the gift you believe you have?
- Do you want to help a friend to develop as a Bible teacher?

If you have said *Yes* to any of these questions, *How to Teach the Bible so that People Meet God* is a great place to start.

ISBN 978-3-95776-035-7
Pb. • 64 pp. • £ 7.50

VTR Publications
info@vtr-online.com
http://www.vtr-online.com

The 5 Habits of Deeply Contented People

Andrew Page

Have you found contentment?
Most people are looking for it.
If you're not, it may be because you've given up...

If you are searching or want to start your search again, *The 5 Habits of Deeply Contented People* is the book for you.

The Bible says that everyone is made in God's image. Andrew Page says there are 5 habits which express that image of God in us. He says "If we can work out what these habits mean in practice for us as individuals, we will experience a deeper level of contentment."

Basing what he writes on the second chapter of the Bible, and making clear that these habits work even if we don't believe in God, Andrew invites his readers to try out the habits for themselves.

- Do you want to be more contented, whatever life throws at you?
- Are you curious to know what it means to be made in God's image?
- Would you like to find out if the 5 habits work?

If you have said Yes to any of these questions, *The 5 Habits of Deeply Contented People* is a great place to start.

ISBN 978-3-95776-009-8
Pb. • 52 pp. • £ 7.00

VTR Publications
info@vtr-online.com
http://www.vtr-online.com

The Matthew Experiment

How Matthew's Gospel can help you know Jesus better

Andrew Page

Are you looking for a new way of getting to know Jesus better? A great place to start is to get into one of the four Gospels. This book is designed to help us to do just that. After writing books about Mark's Gospel and about John's Gospel, Andrew Page has now turned his attention to the Gospel of Matthew.

The Matthew Experiment is two things. First, it's a basic commentary: Andrew unpacks the message of Matthew by teaching through the Gospel from beginning to end. And second, it's an invitation: the book explains how readers can learn the order of the incidents in Matthew, and so try the experiment of using what they have learnt to help them meditate their way through the Gospel. This stems from Andrew's conviction that Matthew wrote not only to give us information about Jesus, but also to help us to meet him.

Would you like to give it a try? If your answer is Yes, The Matthew Experiment is the book for you.

ISBN 978-3-95776-069-2
Pb. • 184 pp. • £ 10.00

VTR Publications
info@vtr-online.com
http://www.vtr-online.com

The John Experiment

How John's Gospel can help you know Jesus better

Andrew Page

Are you looking for a new way into the Gospels? Whether you have been a Christian for many years or are just considering the Christian faith, John's Gospel is a great place to start.

In The John Experiment Andrew Page unpacks John's Gospel and shows you how to commit it to memory. He explains how learning to meditate on the Gospel events is transforming his relationship with Jesus.

Would you like to give it a go? If your answer is Yes, then The John Experiment is the book for you.

ISBN 978-3-95776-070-8
Pb. • 146 pp. • £ 9.50

VTR Publications
info@vtr-online.com
http://www.vtr-online.com

The Mark Experiment

How Mark's Gospel can help you know Jesus better

Andrew Page

If you are looking for a new way into Mark's Gospel and you long to allow the Gospel to help you worship and experience Jesus, *The Mark Experiment* is the book for you.

In *The Mark Experiment* Andrew Page shows you how to commit the Gospel to memory and explains how learning to meditate on the Gospel events has transformed his relationship with Jesus. Think what this might mean for your understanding of the life and ministry of Jesus.

One exciting result of this book has been the development of an innovative drama in which a team of 15 Christians from a church or student group acts out every incident in the Gospel of Mark as theatre-in-the-round. The Mark Drama is now being performed in many countries around the world.

www.themarkdrama.com

ISBN 978-3-937965-21-5
Pb. • 106 pp. • £ 8.00

VTR Publications
info@vtr-online.com
http://www.vtr-online.com

www.ingramcontent.com/pod-product-compliance
Ingram Content Group UK Ltd.
Pitfield, Milton Keynes, MK11 3LW, UK
UKHW021819190726
13853UKWH00003B/1059

9 783957 761309